Nelson Comprehens

Pupil Book

3

Wendy Wren
Series Editor: John Jackman

Nelson Thornes

Published in 2009 by:
Nelson Thornes Ltd
Delta Place
27 Bath Road
CHELTENHAM
GL53 7TH
United Kingdom

13 / 10 9 8 7 6 5

A catalogue record for this book is available from the British Library

ISBN 978 1 4085 0548 9

Illustrations by Gay Galsworthy and Élisabeth Eudes-Pascal at Graham-Cameron
Illustration and Robin Edmonds, Gustavo Mazali, Pedro Penizzotto, Norbert
Sipos, Studio Pulsar and Roger Wade Walker at Beehive Illustration

Photographs courtesy of: Fotolia 24 (all); Getty Images 34,
35, 39, 57; Istock 52 (girl with apple), 53, 56.

Cover illustration by Gustavo Mazali

Page layout by Topics – The Creative Partnership, Exeter

Printed in China by 1010 Printing International Ltd

Acknowledgements

The author and publisher are grateful to the following for permission to reproduce copyright material:

Cambridge University Press for Eric and Tessa Hadley, 'The Storm' from *Legends of Earth, Air, Fire and Water* by Eric
and Tessa Hadley (1985); Express Newspapers for Lucy Johnston and Martyn Halle, 'Outlaw sunbeds plea as cancer
cases soar', *Sunday Express*, 16.11.08; A M Heath & Co Ltd on behalf of the Estates of the authors for material from
Noel Streatfeild, *The Growing Summer*, Collins (1966). Copyright © Noel Streatfeild 1962; and Joan Aiken, *The Wolves
of Willoughby Chase* (1962) pp. 62-3. Copyright © Joan Aiken 1962; Merle Hodge for her story, 'Jeffie Lemmington
and Me'; The Orion Publishing Group for material from Lauren St John, *The White Giraffe*, Orion Children's Books
(2006) pp. 39-42; Penguin Books Ltd for material from James Vance Marshall, *Walkabout* (first published as *The
Children*, Michael Joseph, 1959) pp. 5-6. Copyright © James Vance Marshall 1969; PFD on behalf of the Estate of
the author for Hilaire Belloc, 'Jim Who Ran Away From His Nurse' from *Cautionary Verses* by Hilaire Belloc. Copyright
© Hilaire Belloc 1907; Martin Reed on behalf of the Estate of the author for Vernon Scannell, 'The Apple Raid'.

Every effort has been made to trace the copyright holders but if any have been inadvertently overlooked
the publishers will be pleased to make the necessary arrangements at the first opportunity.

Contents

Trouble for Oliver!
▶ **Understanding the layout conventions of playscripts**

Oliver asks for more

Characters:	Oliver Twist
	Mr Bumble, master of the workhouse
	Boy 1
	Boy 2
	Boy 3
Scene:	The **workhouse.** *A large hall at suppertime. The boys are seated at a long, wooden table. There is a bowl and spoon in front of each of them.*
MR BUMBLE:	Now, boys, let us thank the Good Lord for the food he has kindly given us.
	*[The boys mumble **grace without enthusiasm**. The **gruel** is served.]*
BOY 1:	*(whispering)* I tell you, if I don't get more food, I might just wake up one night and **devour** that skinny boy in the next bed!
BOY 2:	*(slopping a spoonful of gruel back into his bowl)* Look at this muck. Ain't worth eating. Fat old Bumble doesn't eat this muck!
BOY 3:	Well, it's all we get and we're going to have seconds! **It's sorted**. Oliver here is going to ask for more, ain't you Oliver?
OLIVER:	*(Oliver smiles weakly and eats as slowly as he can.)* Ye–es. When I've finished this. I have to finish this first.
BOY 3:	*(threateningly)* Well, be quick about it!
MR BUMBLE:	Have we all finished?
	[The boys whisper to each other and wink at Oliver.]
BOY 3:	*(giving Oliver a **vicious** poke)* Go on then. You drew the short straw. You've got to do it!
	[Oliver gets up from the table with his bowl and spoon. He walks towards Mr Bumble and stops in front of him.]
OLIVER:	Please, Sir, I want some more.
	[Mr Bumble turns pale. He looks in astonishment at Oliver.]
MR BUMBLE:	*(in a faint voice)* What?
OLIVER:	Please, Sir, I want some more.

Scene based on *Oliver Twist* by Charles Dickens

- How many characters are in the scene?
- Where is the scene set?
- How do you know who is speaking?
- Which brackets are used to tell the actors how to 'say' or 'do' something?
- Which brackets are used to 'tell the story'?
- Explain the meaning of the words and phrases in **bold**.
- Why do you think the boys said grace 'without enthusiasm'?
- How do you know Boy 1 is really hungry?
- How do you think Oliver feels when he walks up to Mr Bumble?
- How do you know that Mr Bumble is shocked by what Oliver says?

Oliver and the undertaker

After Oliver had dared to 'ask for more', the people who run the workhouse want rid of him. Mr Bumble takes him to be an apprentice to an undertaker.

Characters:	Oliver Twist Mr Bumble, master of the workhouse Mr Sowerberry, the undertaker Mrs Sowerberry, his wife
Scene:	*The undertaker's shop at dusk.*

[Mr Sowerberry is making some entries in his day-book by the light of a dismal candle when Mr Bumble and Oliver arrive.]

MR SOWERBERRY: Ah! Is that you, Bumble?

MR BUMBLE: No one else, Mr Sowerberry. Here, *(pushing Oliver forward)* I've brought the boy.

[Mr Sowerberry raises the candle above his head and peers at Oliver. Oliver makes a small bow.]

MR SOWERBERRY: Oh, that's the boy, is it? *(He turns to the back of the shop.)* Mrs Sowerberry! Will you have the goodness to come here a moment, my dear?

Understanding the scene
- Who are the characters in the scene?
- Where is the scene set?
- What is Mr Sowerberry doing when Mr Bumble and Oliver arrive?
- Pick out a stage direction that:
    a tells an actor/actress how to say the lines
    b tells an actor/actress what to do
    c relates the story.

Looking at words
Explain the meanings of these words as they are used in the scene:

a undertaker	**b** dusk	**c** dismal
d anxiously	**e** sharply	**f** victuals

[Mrs Sowerberry comes from a room at the back of the shop.]

MR BUMBLE: Good evening, Mrs Sowerberry.

[She ignores Bumble and peers at Oliver. Oliver bows again.]

MR SOWERBERRY: My dear, this is the boy from the workhouse that I told you of.

MRS SOWERBERRY: Dear me, he's very small.

MR BUMBLE: (anxiously) Why, he is rather small. There's no denying it. But he'll grow, Mrs Sowerberry, he'll grow...

MRS SOWERBERRY: (sharply) Ah, I dare say he will on our victuals and our drink. I see no saving in parish children, not I. They always cost more to keep than they're worth. However, men always think they know best!

[Mr Bumble hurriedly backs out of the door.]

MR SOWERBERRY: (fearfully) Now my dear...

MRS SOWERBERRY: There! Get downstairs, little bag o' bones.

[Mrs Sowerberry opens a side door and pushes Oliver down a steep flight of stairs into a damp, dark stone cellar.]

Scene based on *Oliver Twist* by Charles Dickens

Looking at character
- The scene is set 'at dusk'. The only light is 'a dismal candle'. How do you think the playwright wants the audience to feel?
- Why do you think Oliver has nothing to say in this scene?
- Why do you think Mr Bumble:

  a is anxious when Mrs Sowerberry says that Oliver is 'very small'?

  b leaves hurriedly?
- What impression do you get of Mrs Sowerberry?
- How do you think Oliver is feeling when he is pushed down the stairs to the cellar?

Extra

In the next part of the story, Oliver is:
- given some cold meat that has been saved for the dog
- taken back upstairs and told he is to sleep under the counter among the coffins.

Prepare and role-play the next scene of the play. It is set the following morning when Oliver is woken up by Mrs Sowerberry.

Oliver meets the Artful Dodger

Oliver has a terrible time at the undertakers and he decides to run away to London.
He arrives at the town of Barnet and stops to rest.

Characters: Oliver Twist
          The Artful Dodger, a street urchin

Scene: *A street in Barnet*

          [Oliver, tired and hungry, is sitting on a doorstep when a boy stops and stares at him.]

DODGER: What's up with you then?

OLIVER: *(beginning to cry)* I am very hungry and tired. I have walked a long way. I have been walking these seven days.

DODGER: Walking for seven days! Beak's after you, eh?

OLIVER: *(looking surprised)* Isn't a 'beak' a bird's mouth?

DODGER: *(laughing)* You don't know much, do you? The beak's the magistrate. And if you're running from the law, I'm your man!

          [Oliver is about to protest, but Dodger is helping him up.]

DODGER   You want grub and you shall have it!

          [Dodger buys ham and bread at a nearby shop.]

OLIVER: *(eating ravenously)* Thank you, Sir, thank you.

DODGER: *(looking around all the time)* Going to London?

OLIVER: *(between mouthfuls)* Yes, I am.

DODGER: *(slyly)* Got any lodgings?

OLIVER: No.

DODGER: Money?

OLIVER: No. Do you live in London?

DODGER: Yes, when I'm at home. I suppose you need some place to sleep tonight?

OLIVER: *(earnestly)* I do indeed.

DODGER: Don't fret. I know a respectable old gentleman who'll give you lodgings for free. Eat up, and then I'll take you to meet Mr Fagin and the other lads.

Scene based on *Oliver Twist* by Charles Dickens

Understanding the scene

1 What is Oliver doing when he meets the Artful Dodger?

2 Why does the Dodger think Oliver is running away?

3 What does he give Oliver to eat?

4 Besides food, what does Oliver need?

5 Who is the Dodger going to take Oliver to meet?

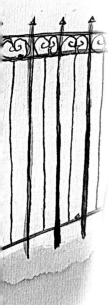

Understanding the words

6 Explain the meaning of these words and phrases as they are used in the scene:

a artful	**b** urchin	**c** magistrate
d running from the law	**e** grub	**f** ravenously
g slyly	**h** earnestly	**i** respectable

Looking at character

7 What impression do you get of the Artful Dodger? What evidence is there that the Artful Dodger might not make a good friend for Oliver? Give evidence for your view.

8 How does Oliver react to the Dodger?

9 Why do you think Oliver is 'eating ravenously'?

10 Why do you think the Dodger is 'looking around' all the time he is questioning Oliver?

Extra

Script a radio interview with Oliver after he has met the Artful Dodger.
Questions should be based on:
- where Oliver was and what he was doing
- how he feels about the Artful Dodger.

The power of advertising

Spend A Pound, Save A Life
Every year, hundreds of dogs are abandoned by their owners. Some are tied up miles from home. Some are thrown out of cars on motorways.
Poppy is just one of them.
Needydogs is a charity that saves these unwanted dogs, gives them a home and cares for them. But we can't do it without your help. Just £1 a month can save Poppy and other mistreated dogs from a lonely, horrible death. Please help by visiting our website:
www.needydogs.co.uk

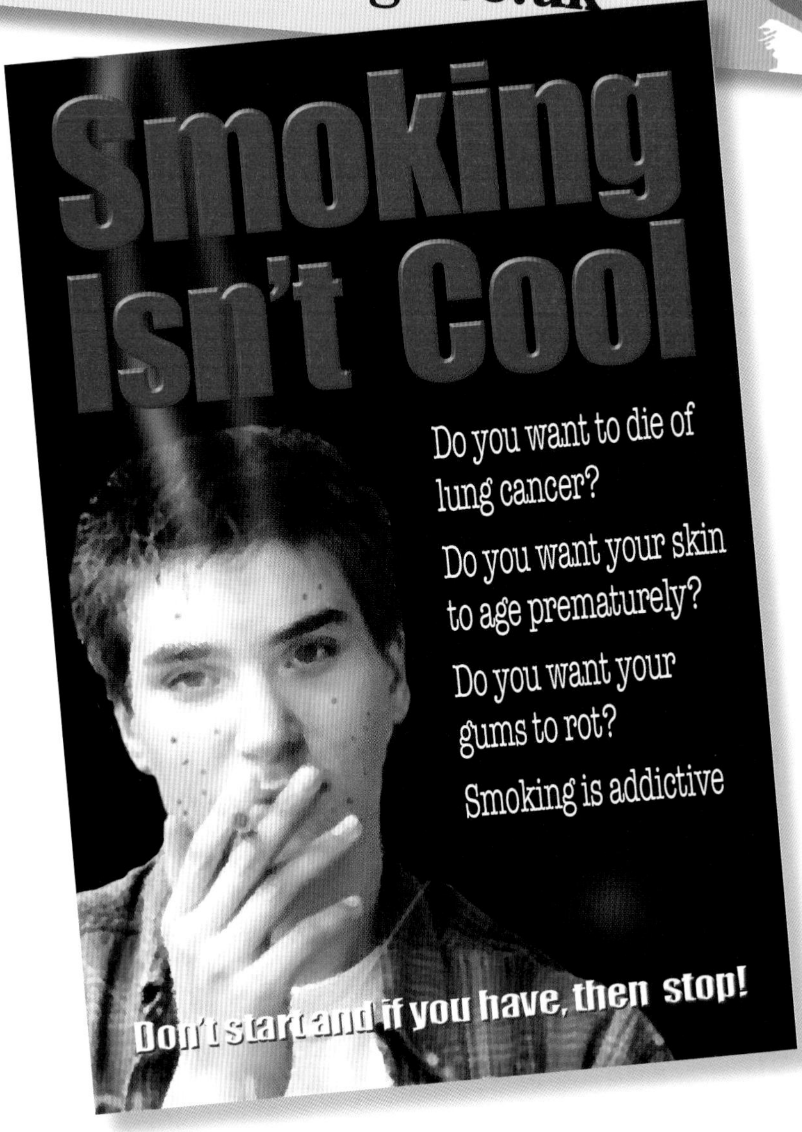
Smoking Isn't Cool
Do you want to die of lung cancer?
Do you want your skin to age prematurely?
Do you want your gums to rot?
Smoking is addictive
Don't start and if you have, then stop!

- Look at each advertisement.
- What is its purpose?
- Who is the audience?
- Where would you expect to see it?
- Explain the meaning of these words: fashionable, funky, trend-setter, abandoned, mistreated, prematurely, addictive.
- What 'emotion' is each advertisement appealing to?
- How has each advertisement used persuasive language, illustration, fonts and colour?
- Which advertisement do you find the most persuasive? Explain your reasons.

The copywriter's job

When we look at an advertisement, we see the finished article. But it begins as an idea that a copywriter has to turn into a successful advert.

Style Sheet 1: Rough layout

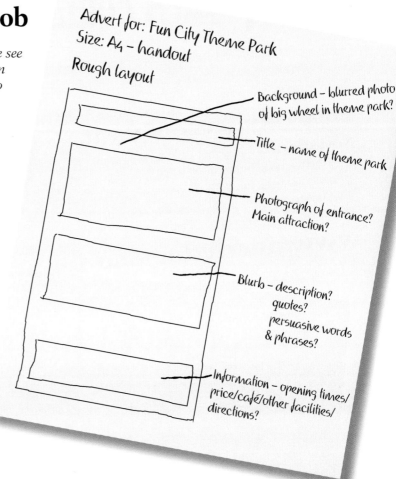

Advert for: Fun City Theme Park
Size: A4 – handout
Rough layout

Background – blurred photo of big wheel in theme park?

Title – name of theme park

Photograph of entrance? Main attraction?

Blurb – description? quotes? persuasive words & phrases?

Information – opening times/ price/café/other facilities/ directions?

Understanding the style sheets

- What is the advertisement for?
- How will people see the advertisement?
- Find two examples of words or phrases used to persuade.
- Find two examples of information.
- What will a group of two adults and two children save by buying a family ticket?

Looking at words

Explain the meaning of these words and phrases as they are used on the style sheets:

a main attraction **b** blurb **c** facilities

d breathtakingly exciting **e** disabled access **f** motorway routes

**Style Sheet 2: Adding detail
to the layout**

Title – blocked caps – colour?
Red / yellow? Heavy black outline?

Illustration – photograph – include people –
happy – enjoying themselves

Blurb –   possible adjectives   amazing
                                        incredible
    black text   thrilling
                                        scary

        persuasive phrases   value for money
                             breathtakingly exciting
    blue text   a must

Info –   opening times 9am to sunset / 364 days a year
    café   light lunch to three course meal
    prices   Adults £10 / children £4 / family ticket for four £25
Also – disabled access
Find us at (check motorway routes)

Exploring further

- Why do you think Style Sheet 1 includes a 'rough layout'?
- Why do you think some items on the style sheets are followed by a question mark and others are not?
- Who do you think the quotes would be from in the blurb?
- Explain what you think the difference between the 'Blurb' and the 'Info' is.
- What do you think happens after the style sheets are finished?

Extra

Using the style sheets and your own ideas, produce an advertisement for
Fun City Theme Park.

25 nights
from
£2,000

Sail Away To The Holiday Of Your Dreams!

This is the chance of a lifetime with prices starting at only £2,000.

Cabin Grade	Price
Inside twin	£2,000
Outside twin	£2,500
Superior outside twin	£2,999
Balcony cabin	£3,400
Balcony suite	£3,999

This is an amazing opportunity to sail in luxury around the sun-drenched islands of the Caribbean on board the world-class *Olympia*.

You will stay in elegant, spacious cabins; enjoy sumptuous meals; and be entertained by world-famous cabaret artists.

Some days will be spent exploring the beautiful, unspoilt islands of St Lucia, Antigua and Barbados. On other days, you can relax aboard and enjoy all that the *Olympia* has to offer as we cruise gently in the crystal waters of the Caribbean.

Places are limited, so book without delay!
Phone 0845 000 000
Visit our website: www.crystalsail.com

Understanding the advertisement

1 What is the purpose of the advertisement?

2 Who is the audience?

3 Give two examples of persuasive words or phrases.

4 Give two examples of information.

Understanding the words

5 Explain the meaning of these words and phrases as they are used in the advertisement:

a luxury   b sun-drenched   c world-class

d spacious   e sumptuous   f crystal waters

g chance of a lifetime   h limited

Exploring the advertisement

6 Why do you think the advertisement begins with:

a the cheapest price   b a photograph of the cruise ship?

7 Look at the words 'luxury', 'elegant' and 'sumptuous'. Why do you think the writer uses these words?

8 What does the writer mean when he says the islands are 'unspoilt'?

9 Why do you think people would pay more for an 'outside twin cabin' than an 'inside twin cabin'?

10 Does the advertisement persuade you that this would be 'The Holiday Of Your Dreams'? Why? Why not?

Extra

Imagine that you are thinking of booking the cruise on the *Olympia* but you want more information. Make a list of questions you will ask when you make the phone call.

Meeting Great-Aunt Dymphna

The Gareth children – Alex, Penny, Robin and Naomi – are sent to stay with their Great-Aunt Dymphna in Ireland. Their first meeting with their Great-Aunt is an alarming experience! They soon realise that they will have to fend for themselves during their stay.

The first impression of Great-Aunt Dymphna was that she was more like an enormous bird than a great-aunt. This was partly because she wore a black cape, which seemed to flap behind her when she moved. Then her nose stuck out of her thin wrinkled old face just like a very hooked beak. On her head she wore a man's tweed hat beneath which straggled wispy white hair. She wore under the cape a shapeless long black dress. On her feet, despite of it being a fine warm evening, were rubber boots.

The children gazed at their great-aunt, so startled by her appearance that the polite greetings they would have made **vanished** from their minds. Naomi was so scared that, though tears went on rolling down her cheeks, she did not make any more noise. Great-Aunt Dymphna had turned her attention to the luggage.

'**Clutter**, clutter! I could never abide clutter. What have you got in all this?' As she said 'this' a rubber boot kicked at the nearest suitcase.

'Clothes, mostly,' said Alex.

'Mummy didn't know what we'd need,' Penny explained, 'so she said we'd have to bring everything.'

'Well, as it's here we must take it home I suppose,' said Great-Aunt Dymphna. 'Bring it to the car,' and she turned and, like a great black eagle, swept out…

'She's as mad as a coot,' Alex whispered to Penny. 'I should think she ought to be in an asylum.'

Penny shivered. 'I do hope other people live close to Reenmore. I don't like us to be alone with her.'

But in Bantry where they stopped to send a **cable** nobody seemed to think Great-Aunt Dymphna mad. It is true the children understood very little of what was said, for they were not used to the Irish **brogue**, but it was clear from the tone of voice used and the expressions on people's faces that what the people of Bantry felt was respect. It came from the man who filled the car up with petrol, and another who put some parcels in the boot.

'Extraordinary!' Alex whispered to Penny when he came out of the hotel. 'When I said "Miss Gareth said it would be all right to send a cable" you'd have thought I said the Queen has said it was all right.'

'Why, what did they say?' Penny asked.

'It was more the way they said it than what they said, but they told me to write down the message and they would telephone it through right away.'

It was beginning to get dark when they left Bantry but as the children peered out of the windows they could just see the purplish mountains, and that the roads had fuchsia hedges instead of ordinary bushes, and that there must be ponds or lakes for often they caught the shimmer of water.

'At least it's awfully pretty,' Penny whispered to Alex. 'Like Mummy said it would be.'

'I can't see how that'll help if she's mad,' Alex whispered back.

Suddenly, without a word of warning, Great-Aunt Dymphna stopped the car.

'We're home.' Then she chuckled. 'I expect you poor little town types thought we'd never make it, but we always do. You'll learn.'

The children stared out of the car windows. Home! They seemed to be in a lonely lane miles from anywhere.

'Get out. Get out,' said Great-Aunt Dymphna. 'There's no drive to the house. It's across that field.'

'Horrible old beast!' thought Alex, dragging their cases from the boot. 'She really is **insufferable**.' But he kept what he felt to himself for out loud all he said was, 'Let's just take the cases we need tonight. We can fetch the others in the morning.'

Alex led the way, carrying his and Naomi's cases. Robin came next. Penny, gripping Naomi's hand, followed the boys. 'I don't wonder nobody brings a telegram here,' said Robin. 'I shouldn't think anybody brings anything. I should think we could all be dead before a doctor comes.'

Alex could have hit him.

From *The Growing Summer*, Noel Streatfeild

- Who are the characters in the story?
- Where does this part of the story take place?
- What does Great-Aunt Dymphna look like?
- What do the **bold** words mean as they are used in the story?
- The children find themselves in a difficult situation: What impression do you get of each of the children? How do they react to Dymphna?
- How do other people react to Dymphna?
- How do you think the author wants you to feel about her?
- How do you feel about her?

Miss Slighcarp

*Miss Slighcarp is governess to Bonnie and her orphaned
cousin Sylvia. When Bonnie's parents go away,
and Miss Slighcarp is left in charge, the
children soon find out she is no ordinary
governess! This part of the story takes
place in the schoolroom.*

The governess, who had been
examining some books on the shelves,
swung round with equal abruptness. She
seemed astonished to see them.

'Where have you been?' she demanded angrily,
after an instant's pause.

'Why,' Sylvia faltered, 'merely in the next room,
Miss Slighcarp.'

But Bonnie, with choking utterance, demanded,
'Why are you wearing my mother's dress?'

Sylvia had observed that Miss Slighcarp had on a
draped gown of old gold velvet with ruby buttons,
far grander than the grey twill she had worn
the day before.

'Don't speak to me in that way, miss!'
retorted Miss Slighcarp in a rage. 'You have

Understanding the passage

● Who are the characters in the story?

● What has Miss Slighcarp done to make Bonnie so angry?

● What happens to the dress and what does Miss Slighcarp
then do to Bonnie?

● Explain the meaning of these words as they are used in the extract:

   a abruptness   **b** astonished   **c** utterance

   d observed   **e** retorted   **f** reckless

   g disposition   **h** insolent   **i** aghast

been spoiled all your life, but we shall soon see who is going to be mistress now. Go to your place and sit down. Do not speak until you are spoken to.'

Bonnie paid not the slightest attention. 'Who said you could wear my mother's best gown?' she repeated. Sylvia, alarmed, had slipped into her place at the table, but Bonnie, reckless with indignation, stood in front of the governess, glaring at her.

'Everything in this house was left entirely to my personal disposition,' Miss Slighcarp said coldly.

'But not her clothes! Not to wear! How dare you? Take it off at once! It's no better than stealing!'

Two white dents had appeared on either side of Miss Slighcarp's nostrils.

'Another word and it's the dark cupboard and bread-and-water for you, miss,' she said fiercely.

'I don't care what you say!' Bonnie stamped her foot. 'Take off my mother's dress!'

Miss Slighcarp boxed Bonnie's ears. Bonnie seized Miss Slighcarp's wrists. In the confusion a bottle of ink was knocked off the table, spilling a long blue trail down the gold velvet skirt. Miss Slighcarp uttered an exclamation of fury.

'Insolent, ungovernable child! You shall suffer for this!' With iron strength she thrust Bonnie into a closet containing crayons, globes and exercise books, and turned the key on her. Then she swept from the room.

Sylvia remained seated, aghast, for half a second. Then she ran to the cupboard door – but alas! Miss Slighcarp had taken the key with her.

From *The Wolves of Willoughby Chase*, Joan Aiken

Looking at character
- What impressions do you get of Bonnie, Sylvia and Miss Slighcarp?
- If you had been in this situation, would you have acted like Bonnie or Sylvia? Give your reasons.

Extra
Choose one of the group to be Miss Slighcarp. The rest of the group question her about the incident with the dress. She wants to appear reasonable and to get you on her side. What questions will you ask? What responses will she give?

Bush Fire!

The story begins late one Friday evening, when three boys are camping in the Australian bush. The weather is very hot and there is a dry north wind. In the middle of the night, Wallace wakes up to find Graham making coffee. Accidentally, Graham knocks over a bottle of methylated spirits, which catches fire.

'It's burning,' howled Graham.

A blue flame snaked from the little heater up through the rocks towards the bottle in the boy's hand; or at least that was how it seemed to happen. It happened so swiftly it may have deceived the eye. Instinctively, to protect himself, Graham threw the bottle away. There was a shower of fire from its neck, as from the nozzle of a hose.

'Oh my gosh,' yelled Wallace and tore off his sleeping-bag. 'Harry!' he screamed. 'Wake up, Harry!'

They tried to stamp on the fire, but their feet were bare and they couldn't find their shoes. They tried to smother it with their sleeping-bags, but it seemed to be everywhere. Harry couldn't even escape from his bag; he couldn't find the zip fastener, and for a few awful moments in his confusion between sleep and wakefulness he thought he was in his bed at home and the house had burst into flames around him. He couldn't come to grips with the situation; he knew only dismay and the wildest kind of alarm. Graham and Wallace, panicking, were throwing themselves from place to place, almost sobbing, beating futilely at the widening arc of fire. Every desperate blow they made seemed to fan the fire, to scatter it farther, to feed it.

'Put it out,' shouted Graham. 'Put it out.'

It wasn't dark any longer. It was a flickering world of tree trunks and twisted boughs, of scrub and saplings and stones, of shouts and wind and smoke and frantic fear. It was so quick. It was terrible.

'Put it out,' cried Graham, and Harry fought out of his sleeping-bag, knowing somehow that they'd never get it out by beating at it, that they'd have to get water up from the creek. But all they had was a four-pint billy-can.

The fire was getting away from them in all directions, crackling through the scrub down-wind, burning fiercely back into the wind. Even the ground was burning: grass, roots and fallen leaves were burning, humus was burning. There were flames on the trees, bark was burning, foliage was flaring, flaring like a whip-crack; and the heat was savage and searing and awful to breathe.

'We can't, we can't,' cried Wallace. 'What are we going to do?'

'Oh, gee,' sobbed Graham. He was crying and he hadn't cried since he was twelve years old. 'What have I done? *We've got to get it out!*'

Harry was scrambling around wildly, bundling all their things together. It was not just that he was more level-headed than the others; it was just that he could see the end more clearly, the hopelessness of it, the absolute certainty of it, the imminent danger of encirclement, the possibility that they might be burnt alive. He could see all this because he hadn't been in it at the start. He wasn't responsible; he hadn't done it; and now he was wide awake he could see more clearly. He screamed at them, 'Grab your stuff and run for it.' But they didn't hear him or didn't want to hear him. They were blackened, their feet were cut, even their hair was singed. They beat and beat, and the fire was leaping into the tree-tops, and there were no black shadows left, only bright light, red light, yellow light, light that was hard and cruel and terrifying, and there was a rushing sound, a roaring sound, explosions, and smoke, smoke like a hot red fog.

'No,' cried Graham. 'No, no, no.' His arms dropped to his sides and he shook with sobs and Wallace dragged him away. 'Oh, Wally,' he sobbed. 'What have I done?'

'We've got to get out of here,' shouted Harry. 'Grab the things and run.'

'Our shoes!' cried Wallace. 'Where are they?'

'I don't know. I don't know.'

'We've got to find our shoes.'

'They'll kill us,' sobbed Graham. 'They'll kill us. It's a terrible thing, an awful thing to have done.'

'Where'd we put our shoes?' Wallace was running around in circles, blindly. He didn't really know what he was doing. Everything had happened so quickly, so suddenly.

'For Pete's sake run!' shouted Harry.

From *Ash Road*, Ivan Southall

 Understanding the passage

1 Who are the characters in the story?

2 What are they doing?

3 At first, how did they try to put out the fire?

4 When Harry woke up, what did he think had happened?

5 What was it that Harry knew they needed to put out the fire?

Looking at words

6 Explain the meaning of these words and phrases as they are used in the extract:
   a instinctively
   b futilely
   c encirclement
   d deceived the eye
   e come to grips with

Looking at character

7 Who is thinking more clearly when the fire starts: Graham or Wallace? Find evidence to support your view.

8 Find evidence in the passage that Graham and Wallace panic as the fire spreads. Think about: what the author tells us; what the boys do and say.

9 Graham says, 'We've got to get it out.' Harry says, 'We've got to get out of here.' How is each boy reacting to the situation? Explain in your own words why Graham and Harry are reacting so differently.

Extra

Choose one of the characters in the passage and retell the incident from his point of view. Remember to include your character's thoughts and feelings as well as what happened.

How to use Booksbooks – your online bookshop

Task: Find and buy *The Secret Garden* by Frances Hodgson Burnett.

Instructions

1 Go to the hyperlink http://www.booksbooks.co.uk. This will bring up the Homepage with a list of **options**.

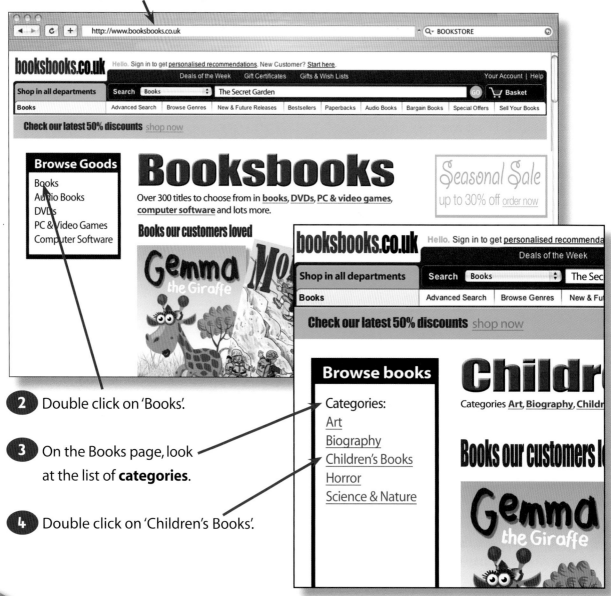

2 Double click on 'Books'.

3 On the Books page, look at the list of **categories**.

4 Double click on 'Children's Books'.

5 Look at the top of the Children's Books page. You will see:

6 Type *The Secret Garden* here: **7** Click on GO.

8 This page will show you all the different **editions** and prices.

£10.99   £8.99   £5.99   £3.99   £2.99

9 Click on the edition that you want to buy.

10 This page will give you details of the book you have **selected**.

11 If you want to buy it, click on BUY NOW.

> - What is Booksbooks?
> - What does it sell?
> - Which category does *The Secret Garden* come under?
> - If you bought the selected book, how much would you pay?
> - Explain the meaning of the words in **bold** as they are used on the web page.
> - Explain why you think the instructions:
>   - are numbered
>   - are written in short, simple sentences
>   - include diagrams.
> - Do you think these instructions are easy to follow or not? Explain your reasons.
> - Compare shopping for a book in a bookshop with shopping for a book online. List the advantages and disadvantages of both.

How to download photographs to your desktop

You will need:

- a PC

- a digital camera memory card

- a USB card reader.

Instructions

1 Switch on the computer.

2 Plug the USB CARD READER into the USB PORT.

3 Place the digital camera MEMORY CARD into the card reader.

Understanding the instructions
- What are the instructions for?
- How many instructions are there?
- What equipment do you need?
- What is on the USB card reader?

Looking at words
Explain the meaning of these words as they are used in the instructions:
a port   **b** select   **c** download   **d** icon   **e** desktop

4 Select OPEN FOLDER TO VIEW FILES.

5 Press OK.

6 Select DCIM FOLDER (Digital Camera images).

7 Select the folder containing the photograph you want to download.

8 Select the photograph.

9 Select COPY 2 icon.

10 Select DESKTOP icon.

11 Press SAVE.

Your photograph is now saved on your desktop.

Exploring further
- Make a list of the features of instructional writing that you can find in these instructions.
- If someone had not downloaded photographs before, do you think these instructions would be easy or difficult to follow? Explain your reasons.
- Once you have stored your photographs on your computer, what could you do to share them with other people?

Extra
Photographs can be printed and kept in albums, or kept or stored on a computer. Discuss and list the advantages and disadvantages of both these methods of storing photographs.

Alarm clock

Most mobile phones can be set like an alarm clock.

Instructions to set the alarm

1

Unlock your phone by pressing the SELECT KEY followed by the HASH KEY.

2

Use the SELECT KEY to get into MENU.

3

On the MENU screen, scroll down using the DIRECTION KEY and choose ORGANISER.

4

On the ORGANISER screen, scroll down using the DIRECTION KEY and choose ALARM CLOCK.

5

Switch the alarm on by using the left or right DIRECTION KEY.

6

Use the bottom DIRECTION KEY to scroll down to the alarm time.

7

Use the NUMBER KEYS to enter the time you want the alarm to go off.

8

Press the CLOSE KEY and you will be asked 'SAVE CHANGES?'

9

Press the SELECT KEY and 'ALARM SAVED' will appear.

 Understanding the instructions

1 What are the instructions for?

2 How many instructions are there?

3 What key do you use to scroll down the MENU screen?

4 What keys do you use to set the time?

Understanding the words

5 Explain the meaning of these words and phrases as they are used in the instructions:

  a hash key   **b** menu   **c** scroll down

Exploring further

6 Why do you think the intructions are numbered?

7 Why do you think the instructions include diagrams?

8 Why do you think some words are in capitals?

9 Think of at least three reasons why you might want to set an alarm on your mobile phone.

10 Do you think these instructions are easy to follow or not? Explain your reasons.

Extra

Think of a piece of equipment you use at home or at school.

Write a set of simple instructions for one of its functions.

The Sword and the Stone

When the service was over they all **passed out of** the church and went into the churchyard, where they beheld a wonderful sight.

A great square stone lay there, and in the stone was an **anvil**, and through anvil and stone was a sword. About the sword were written in letters of gold these words: 'He who pulleth this sword out of this stone and anvil is the rightly born King of England.'

When all the lords saw these words they tried, one after another, to pull the sword out of the stone. But no one was able to move it from its place. 'He is not here,' said the Archbishop, 'who can draw out the sword. I do not doubt, however, but God will make him known. Let us **appoint** ten knights, men of good fame, to keep watch over the sword.'

Then they agreed among themselves to meet on a future day, and to let any man who wished try his skill at withdrawing the sword. The Archbishop arranged that on New Year's Day there should be a **tournament**, and other fine doings, that the lords and commons should be kept together till the King should be revealed.

So upon New Year's Day the lords came together; and among them rode Sir Ector, a noble knight and one who had loved King Uther well, and in his company his son Sir Kay (who had received his knighthood but last Hallowmass), and young Arthur, his adopted son, who was but a youth.

As they rode to the place of meeting, Sir Kay found that he had left his sword behind at their lodging, and he asked young Arthur to ride back and bring it for him.

'Right gladly will I do that,' said the boy. 'Haste you on with our father. I will return to the town with all speed and will bring your sword.'

When he reached their lodging he knocked hard at the door, but no one answered, for they had all gone to the tournament.

Arthur was angry, and said to himself: 'I will ride to the churchyard and take the sword from the stone, for I do not wish my brother to be without a sword this day.'

When he came to the churchyard he **alighted** from his horse, and, going to the anvil, lightly pulled the sword out of the stone; and, mounting his horse again, he rode as fast as he could back to Sir Kay and gave him the sword.

Sir Kay grasped the sword, well pleased. **His eye ran down it**, and he knew it was the sword from the stone. He hastened to rejoin his father and tell him the news.

'Sir,' cried he, when he came up to Sir Ector, 'surely I, and none other, am chosen to be King of England, since in my hand I bear the sword of the stone!'

Sir Ector led his son and the boy Arthur into the church, and commanded his son to tell him truly how he had got the sword.

Sir Kay's **face fell**, but he answered stoutly:

'My brother Arthur brought it to me.'

Then said Sir Ector to Arthur, 'Tell me, did you **pluck** the sword from the stone?'

Arthur at once confessed how, when he had reached home, he had found no one in the house to give him his brother's sword, so he had made all haste to the churchyard and plucked the sword from the stone that rested there.

'Were none there,' asked Sir Ector, 'to **forbid** the act?'

'Nay,' said the boy, 'they had gone, every one, to the tournament.'

This was true, for the knights had gone to try their skill.

Then said Sir Ector to Arthur: 'I know well you must be King of the land.'

'Wherefore should I be King?' asked Arthur.

'Sir,' was Ector's reply, 'it is clearly **ordained**. For the man who can draw the sword out of the stone shall be rightful King of this land.'

From *King Arthur and His Knights*, anonymous

- What was in the churchyard?
- What was going to happen on New Year's Day?
- What do we know about Arthur?
- Why did Arthur pull the sword from the stone?
- What do the **bold** words and phrases mean as they are used in the extract?
- Why do you think all the Lords tried to pull the sword from the stone?
- What impression do you get of Arthur and Sir Kay?
- Arthur was Sir Ector's 'adopted' son. Who do you think Arthur's real father might have been?
- Do you think Arthur will be a 'hero' or a 'villain' in the rest of the story?

Krishna and Kaliya

Krishna is a Hindu god, and legend has it that he was brought up in a cowherd's family. There are many myths about him. In this story, he defeats the Serpent King.

Krishna and his friends loved to play by the Yamuna river. On long summer days, while the cows were grazing close by, Krishna and the other boys would play throwing and catching a ball, tossing it high in the air and leaping strenuously to make sure it did not fall in the water.

For in the water was great danger. This stretch of the river was home to a serpent. Kaliya was an evil serpent that had many heads and could breathe terrible fire.

One day, while the boys were playing, Krishna climbed up a tree that hung over the riverbank. 'Throw the ball to me,' he cried.

One of his friends called out, 'Be careful! You are too close to the water!'

'Throw me the ball,' Krishna repeated.

Understanding the story
- What did Krishna and his friends do on 'long summer days'?
- What was extraordinary about Kaliya?
- Where did Kaliya live?
- Why did Krishna leap into the river?
- How did Krishna defeat the serpent?

Looking at words
Explain the meanings of these words and phrases as they are used in the story:

a strenuously **b** grasp   **c** dismay   **d** retrieve   **e** bolted
f awaiting   **g** merciful **h** destructive **i** banished

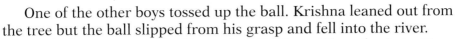

One of the other boys tossed up the ball. Krishna leaned out from the tree but the ball slipped from his grasp and fell into the river.

The boys groaned in dismay but Krishna did not hesitate. He leaped in the river to retrieve the ball. The other boys watched fearfully. For a moment there was complete silence, then a deafening roar came from the water as Kaliya rose up. Its many terrible heads thrashed about and fire and smoke poured from its many mouths.

The cows bolted in panic and the boys sprang back, shrieking and crying, so great was their fear. 'Where is Krishna?' one of them cried.

'He must surely be dead,' wailed another. 'The serpent has killed him!'

But Krishna was not dead. Kaliya had wrapped his body around the young boy but Krishna fought back and began attacking each of the serpent's heads in turn. He could make himself as heavy as the whole world and with this weight he danced on the heads of the serpent.

Kaliya's heads began to die one by one. The serpent realised that Krishna was no ordinary boy and that he could not defeat him. When he had no strength left, Kaliya became still, awaiting certain death.

But Krishna was merciful as well as strong. He knew that it was the nature of a serpent to be violent so he stopped his destructive dance and pardoned the creature. He banished him from the river and Kaliya slunk away, grateful to have escaped with his life.

Exploring further
- What impression do you get of: **a** Krishna **b** Kaliya?
- When the ball fell into the water, why do you think the boys 'groaned in dismay'?
- Why did the serpent realise that Krishna was 'no ordinary boy'?
- Explain in your own words why Krishna spared the serpent's life.
- What makes Krishna the 'hero' of the story?

Extra

Discuss other stories, films or TV programmes you know where the hero/heroine defeats an evil monster.

Why do you think stories like this are so popular?

The Storm

Once a rich mandarin was saved from a fierce storm at sea by a light that guided him to the safety of an island. The people of the island told him that the light was the lantern of the Lin maiden. This is the sad story the people of the island told the mandarin.

'…Hundreds of years ago, on the shore of the eastern sea, there lived a fisher family named Lin: a father, a mother, two sons, and a daughter – and such a daughter, known and loved along the whole coast. She was up first every morning to make breakfast for her parents. Then down to the sea with her father and brothers to help prepare the boats and nets. Every morning as they launched their boats against the incoming waves they heard her call, "Good wind and good weather!"

'Sir, you're beginning to dream by that warm fire, and perhaps it's the storm which fills your mind. That's how it was with the Lin maiden. She had been working with her mother one day. They'd had their midday meal and as she sat she began to feel sleepy, and she dreamed a strange dream.

'She dreamed of the five dragon brothers who live beneath the sea. Something had made them angry – and when they are angry, they lash their mile-long tails, mountains collapse into the sea and waves touch the sky.

'The fierce storm raged in her dream, and there, tossed about in their little boats, she saw her father and her brothers. She rushed to the seashore and waded into the water, and somehow she caught hold of the rope fastened to the bows of her father's boat. Holding this rope in her teeth she seized the ropes tied to her brothers' boats and began to pull them all to safety.

'Just then, her mother tried to wake her. "Daughter! Daughter!"

'The Lin maiden opened her mouth to answer, and in her dream the rope slipped from between her teeth and her father's boat disappeared under the waves.

'All through the afternoon, far into the evening, mother and daughter sat waiting, for what they knew must come. Only two brothers returned. "Our father's boat has been lost. He has gone to the Sea Dragon's Palace."

'The Lin maiden said nothing. She ran past her brothers and out of the house, down to the seashore; and there she plunged into the water to seek for her lost father…

'They never found the body, sir. But her brothers and other sailors started to see her out at sea, in the fiercest storms. No sailor who sees her is ever lost. They come safely to shore, as you did tonight, sir, with the help of her lantern.'

'The Storm' from *Legends of Earth, Air, Fire and Water* by Eric and Tessa Hadley

Understanding the story

1 What did the Lin maiden do every morning?

2 What did the five dragon brothers do when they were angry?

3 In her dream, how did the Lin maiden hold on to the ropes of her father's boat and her brothers' boats?

4 What happened when her mother woke her up?

5 When she realised her father was lost, what did the Lin maiden do?

Looking at words

6 Explain the meaning of these words as they are used in the story:
   a launched   **b** lash   **c** collapse
   d seized   **e** plunged   **f** lantern

Looking at character

7 What impression do you get of the Lin maiden?

8 Why do you think she called out, 'Good wind and good weather' when the boats were launched?

9 How do you think the dream made her feel?

10 How do you think she and her mother felt as they waited 'through the afternoon and far into the evening'?

11 Do you think the Lin maiden is the heroine of the story? Explain your reasons.

Extra

The mother and daughter waited all afternoon and evening for the men to come back. What do you think they said to each other? Write their conversation.

An Egyptian Treasure!

GREAT FIND AT THEBES, LORD CARNARVON'S LONG QUEST.

From Our Cairo Correspondent, Valley of the Kings (by runner to Luxor), Nov 29.

This afternoon Lord Carnarvon and Mr Howard Carter **revealed** to a large company what promises to be the most **sensational** Egyptological discovery of the century.

The find consists of, among other objects, the funeral **paraphernalia** of the Egyptian King Tutankhamen, one of the famous **heretic** kings of the Eighteenth Dynasty.

The remarkable discovery announced to-day is the reward of patience, perseverance and **perspicacity**. For nearly sixteen years Lord Carnarvon, with the assistance of Mr Howard Carter, has been carrying out **excavations** on the part of the site of ancient Thebes situated on the west bank of the Nile at Luxor. Seven years ago work was started in the Valley of the Kings, after other excavators had abandoned the Valley. The search was continued systematically, and at last the dogged perseverance of Mr Carter, his thoroughness, above all his *flair*, were rewarded by the discovery. Mr Carter covered up the site and telegraphed to Lord Carnarvon, who at once came out from England.

The sealed outer door was carefully opened: then a way was cleared down some sixteen steps along a passage of about 25ft. The door to the chamber was found to be sealed as the outer door had been. With difficulty an entrance was effected, and when the last the excavators managed to squeeze their way in an extraordinary sight met their eyes, one that they could **scarcely credit**.

THE TREASURE WITHIN

First they saw three magnificent State couches, all gilt, with exquisite carving. On these rested beds, beautifully carved, gilt, inlaid with ivory and semi-precious stones and also innumerable boxes of exquisite workmanship. One of these boxes was inlaid with ebony and ivory, with gilt inscriptions; another contained **emblems** of the underworld; on a third, which contained Royal robes, handsomely embroidered, precious stones, and golden sandals, were beautifully painted hunting scenes.

There was a stool of ebony inlaid with ivory, with the most delicately carved duck's feet: also a child's stool of fine workmanship. Beneath one of the couches was the State Throne of King Tutankhamen, probably one of the most beautiful objects of art ever discovered. There was also a heavily gilt chair, with portraits of the King and Queen, the whole encrusted with turquoise, carnelian, lapis and other semi-precious stones.

Two life-sized bituminised statues of the King, with gold work holding a golden stick and mace, faced each other, the handsome features, the feet, and the hands delicately carved, with eyes of glass and head-dress richly studded with gems.

There were also four chariots, the sides of which were encrusted with semi-precious stones and rich gold decoration. These were dismantled, with a charioteer's apron of leopard skin hanging over the seat.

› Where would you expect to find an article like this?

› What is the article about?

› Name three things that were found in the tomb.

› Explain the meanings of the **bold** words and phrases as they are used in the article.

› Would the headline make you want to read the article? Why? Why not?

› What impression do you get of Howard Carter?

› Why do you think 'other excavators had abandoned the Valley'?

› Why do you think the chariots had been 'dismantled'?

› There are eight paragraphs in the article. Say briefly what each is about.

35

Treasures of the past

This is a transcript of a radio programme where the interviewer, Fiona Jacobs, talks to an expert in archaeology.

Fiona Jacobs: Good evening. I'm Fiona Jacobs and you are listening to Treasures of the Past, a series of programmes that looks at astounding archaeological discoveries. Tonight, I'm joined by Professor Simon Black, an expert on Ancient Egypt, and we'll be discussing the discovery of Tutankhamen's tomb. Good evening, Professor Black.

Simon Black: Good evening.

Fiona Jacobs: Most people know about the amazing treasures Howard Carter found in the first chamber of the tomb, but why was he so sure there was a second chamber?

Simon Black: Well, as Carter says in his biography, among all the treasures 'there was no coffin or trace of a mummy'. So they looked for and found another sealed doorway between two life-sized figures of the King.

Fiona Jacobs: And that's where they found the mummy?

Simon Black: Yes. But this doorway had a hole in it and Carter was worried that tomb-robbers had got there first.

Fiona Jacobs: Did Carter get through this sealed doorway immediately?

Simon Black: No. There were so many precious objects in the first chamber that it took seven weeks to clear it. Carter likened it to 'a gigantic game of spillikins'. They had to be so careful not to damage the objects as they removed them.

Understanding the interview

- Who is: **a** the interviewer? **b** the interviewee?
- What is the radio programme called?
- Why was Carter sure there was a second chamber?
- Why was he worried that 'the tomb-robbers had got there first'?
- Why did they need a hoist to remove the lid?
- Find an example of:
  a a quote of what Howard Carter actually said
  b reported speech of Howard Carter's words.

Looking at words
Explain the meanings of these words and phrases as they are used in the interview:

a astounding   **b** biography   **c** mummy   **d** precious   **e** manual labour
f sarcophagus   **g** hoist   **h** shrouds   **i** effigy

Fiona Jacobs: So, after seven weeks, Carter was ready to break through into the burial chamber. What did he find?

Simon Black: The first thing he saw, about a yard in front of the hole he had made in the door, was a wall of gold. This turned out to be a huge shrine with three more inside it, you know, like Russian dolls. Carter said that it took 84 days of real manual labour to demolish the wall between the two chambers and dismantle the shrines.

Fiona Jacobs: So when did Carter actually see the now-famous death mask of King Tutankhamen?

Simon Black: In February, 1924. The sarcophagus was huge, 9ft in length. Carter rigged up a hoist to remove the lid that weighed over a ton and a quarter. When the lid was removed – well, let me tell you in Carter's own words: 'The light shone on the sarcophagus. The lid being suspended in mid air, we rolled back the covering shrouds, one by one, and as the last was removed, a gasp of wonderment escaped our lips, so gorgeous was the sight that met our eyes: a golden effigy of the young boy-king, of most magnificent workmanship filled the whole of the sarcophagus'. Carter was the first person to look on the face of the Pharaoh for over 3000 years.

Fiona Jacobs: A fascinating story, Professor Black. Thank you.

Exploring further
- What do you think Carter meant when he said that removing the objects was like 'a gigantic game of spillikins'?
- Explain why the shrines are described as being 'like Russian dolls'.
- Based on the evidence of Carter's own words at the end of the interview, how do you think everyone felt when the shrouds were removed?
- How do you think you would have felt, looking at the face of Tutankhamen and knowing that you were the first to see it for over 3000 years?
- Can you think of other 'treasures' that the radio station could make programmes about?

Extra
Imagine you could meet Howard Carter. What questions would you like to ask him?

THE VALLEY OF THE KINGS

The Valley of the Kings lies on the west bank of the River Nile. To date, approximately 80 tombs have been excavated there, the most famous of which is the tomb of Tutankhamen. The Pharaohs of Egypt abandoned the practice of building pyramids as they were plundered by tomb robbers. Instead, secret tombs were dug out of the rock in the valley and the pharaohs were buried with swords, games, writing tools, oil lamps, beds, chairs – in fact everything they would need in the after-life. The tombs were then sealed and anyone who knew where they were, sworn to secrecy.

Tutankhamen was only 10 years old when he became Egypt's king. His death, in his teens, is still something of a mystery. Examination of his skull shows damage that has led some people to believe he was murdered by a blow to the head. The skeleton shows evidence of a broken leg, prompting some to say that blood poisoning from the wound was the cause of death.

However he died, his death was clearly sudden and unexpected. His tomb was too small ever to have been intended for a king when compared to that of other Pharaohs, such as Rameses II.

See also:
• The Life of Howard Carter   • Tutankhamen's Death Mask

Cairo
Egypt
Valley of the Kings   Luxor

Visit the
Valley
of the
Kings
www.pharaohlandtours.co.uk

VISIT
EGYPT
www.pharaohlandhotels.co.uk

Understanding the web page

1 Where is the Valley of the Kings?

2 How many tombs have been excavated? Give two examples of things found in them.

3 How old was Tutankhamen when he became King?

4 How do people think he died?

5 The article has three paragraphs. Briefly say what each is about.

Understanding the words

6 Explain the meaning of these words and phrases as they are used in the web page:

a to date   **b** excavated   **c** plundered

d after-life   **e** sworn to secrecy   **f** prompting

Exploring the web page

7 What evidence is there that Tutankhamen's death was 'unexpected'?

8 Look at the sections at the top of the page. What would you expect to find if you clicked on:

a Photos   **b** Bookshop   **c** Site Map

9 Why are some of the words on the web page underlined?

10 Why do you think the page has advertisements for hotels and tours in Egypt?

Extra

• Choose one of the underlined words on the web page.

• Research it using the web or a library. Make notes.

• Prepare a report to read to the class.

Let me tell you a story
▸ **Telling stories through poetry**

Jim
Who Ran Away From His Nurse, And Was Eaten By A Lion

There was a boy whose name was Jim;
His friends were very good to him.
They gave him tea, and cakes, and jam,
And slices of delicious ham,
And chocolate with pink inside,
And little tricycles to ride,
And read him stories **through and through**,
And even took him to the Zoo –
But there it was the dreadful **fate**
Befell him, which I now **relate**.

You know – at least you ought to know,
For I have often told you so –
That children never are allowed
To leave their nurses in a crowd;
Now this was Jim's especial **foible**,
He ran away when he was able,
And on this **inauspicious** day
He slipped his hand and ran away!
He hadn't gone a yard when – Bang!
With open jaws, a lion sprang,
And hungrily began to eat
The boy: beginning at his feet.

Now, just imagine how it feels
When first your toes and then your heels,
And then by gradual degrees,
Your shins and ankles, calves and knees,
Are slowly eaten, bit by bit.
No wonder Jim **detested** it!
No wonder that he shouted 'Hi!'
The honest keeper heard his cry,
Though very fat he almost ran
To help the little gentleman.
'Ponto!' he ordered as he came
(For Ponto was the lion's name),
'Ponto!' he cried, with angry frown.

'Let go, Sir! Down, Sir! Put it down!'
The lion made a sudden stop,
He let the dainty **morsel** drop,
And **slunk reluctant** to his cage,
Snarling with disappointed rage,
But when he bent him over Jim,
The honest keeper's eyes were dim.
The lion having reached his head,
The miserable boy was dead!

When Nurse informed his parents, they
Were more concerned than I can say: –
His Mother, as she dried her eyes,
Said, 'Well – it gives me no surprise,
He would not do as he was told!'
His Father, who was self-controlled,
Bade all the children round **attend**
To James's miserable end,
And always keep a-hold of Nurse
For fear of finding something worse.

'Jim Who Ran Away From His Nurse,
And Was Eaten By A Lion' from *Cautionary Tales for Children*,
Hilaire Belloc (this edition from *The Nation's Favourite
Children's Poems*)

- Who is the main character in the poem?

- How do you know that his friends were 'very good to him'?

- What other characters are introduced as the story is told?

- Where was the main character when something 'dreadful' happened?

- Explain the meaning of the words and phrases in **bold** as they are used in the poem.

- Find phrases where the poet talks directly to the reader.

- Why do you think he does this?

- What impression do you get of:
  - the Nurse
  - the Keeper
  - Jim's mother and father?

- Do you think the poem is 'serious' or 'funny'? Explain your reasons.

The Apple-Raid

Darkness came early, though not yet cold;
Stars were strung on the telegraph wires;
Street lamps spilled pools of liquid gold;
The breeze was spiced with garden fires.

That smell of burnt leaves, the early dark,
Can still excite me but not as it did
So long ago when we met in the park –
Myself, John Peters and David Kidd.

We moved out of town to the district where
The lucky and wealthy had their homes
With garages, gardens, and apples to spare
Ripely clustered in the trees' green domes.

We chose this place we meant to plunder
And climbed the wall and dropped down to
The secret dark. Apples crunched under
Our feet as we moved through the grass and dew.

 Understanding the poem

● Who 'met in the park'?
● What did they do?
● From what part of the tree did they steal the fruit?
● How did they carry it?
● How do you know that what the poet is describing happened a long time ago?

Looking at words

Explain the meaning of these words and phrases as they are used in the poem:

a spiced   **b** district   **c** clustered   **d** plunder   **e** loot   **f** lies cold

The clusters on the lower boughs of the tree
Were easy to reach. We stored the fruit
In pockets and jerseys until all three
Boys were heavy with their tasty loot.

Safe on the other side of the wall
We moved back to town and munched as we went.
I wonder if David remembers at all
That little adventure, the apples' fresh scent.

Strange to think that he's fifty years old,
That tough little boy with scabs on his knees;
Stranger to think that John Peters lies cold
In an orchard in France beneath apple trees.

'The Apple-Raid', Vernon Scannell

Exploring further
● In which season of the year do you think the apple-raid took place? Give your
  reasons.
● Why do you think the boys went 'out of town' to steal apples?
● Look at these descriptions: 'liquid gold', 'green domes', 'the secret dark'.
  a Say what each is describing.
  b Do you think it is a good description? Why? Why not?
● Why do you think John Peters 'lies cold' in France?
● How do you think the poet feels when he remembers 'that little adventure'?

Extra
Act out the poem from when the boys meet in the park to when they return to
town. Think about what the boys would say and do during 'that little adventure'.

Early Last Sunday Morning

Early last Sunday morning
Dad announced we needed a glass of fresh air
and a mouthful of greenness.
So we slipped off to the nearby park
where we crept in as soundless as snails.
Around us the day breathed air
that was as sharp as vinegar
reminding us that winter was well on its way.

Inside we watched the trees stretch and wake
while the grass stood up and shivered.
Soon I was pointing towards a spider
that was strung on a necklace web
while far behind it
the sun rolled out like a golden ball.

Suddenly Dad smiled
as a squirrel scampered from a bush
then turned to grey stone
until with a flick of its tail
it waved goodbye and was gone.

Later as we passed the children's playground
I looked at the lonely, red slide
and briefly remembered the summer days
when I flew its slippery, red tongue.
But a tug of wind pushed me past
Until I just let the warmth in Dad's hand
finally lead me on towards home.

'Early Last Sunday Morning', Ian Souter

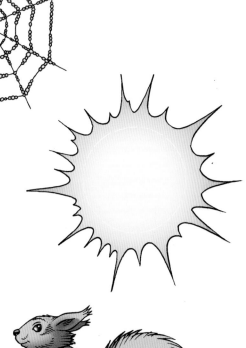

Understanding the poem

1 What is the setting for the poem?

2 Who are the characters in the poem?

3 In what season does the poem take place?

4 What living things does the poet see?

5 What has the poet played on in the children's playground?

Understanding the words

6 Explain the meaning of these words and phrases as they are used in the poem:
  a announced   **b** well on its way   **c** scampered
  d flick   **e** briefly   **f** tug

Exploring the poem

7 Explain in your own words why Dad thought it was a good idea to go to the park.

8 Look at these similes: 'soundless as snails', 'sharp as vinegar'.
  a What is each simile describing?
  b Do you think they are good descriptions? Why? Why not?

9 What does the poet mean when he:
  a says that the squirrel 'turned to grey stone';
  b describes the slide as 'lonely'?

10 How do you think the poet felt about the trip to the park with his Dad? Explain your reasons.

Extra

Imagine that you are the poet. Write a short description of what you did and how you felt 'early last Sunday morning'.

A new school

Next morning Martine woke feeling as if she was going to the dentist. For a long time she lay there with her eyes screwed tightly shut, because that way she could pretend that none of it had happened. Her home had not burned down, and her mum and dad were not gone forever, and she had not been sent to the wilds of Africa to live with a total stranger. Finally, when she could avoid it no longer, she opened her eyes. A **vast** sky of the most **incredible** blue filled her vision. The clock on the bedside table said 6.05 a.m. Right on cue, an orange-breasted bird fluttered onto a thatch beam outside her window and began singing a song of pure happiness. *Tirrootiree, tirrootiree.*

Propping herself up on one elbow, Martine gazed out over the game reserve. The waterhole was draped with early morning mist and streaked with gold from the sun. A dozen or so elephants were splashing around in it, **wallowing** in the mud and spraying each other with their trunks. Zebras were grazing nearby. She shook her head in wonder. The scene didn't take away the **anguish** in her heart, but it definitely helped.

Even so, she walked downstairs on leaden feet. Her grandmother was sitting at the kitchen table, her hands wrapped around a coffee mug. When Martine entered, she stood up quickly and said: 'Good morning, Martine, I hope you slept well.' Her voice shook slightly, as though she was nervous. Before Martine could speak, she went on hurriedly: 'There is a boiled egg in the pan and some bread in the toaster and anything else you might need on the kitchen table. On the counter over there, you'll find a lunchbox containing sunscreen, yellow cling peaches from the garden and some cheese and chutney sandwiches. I have to go out now to feed the young elephant, but I'll be back at 7.30 to take you to school.'

Martine was still stammering a thank you when the stable door banged behind her grandmother and a gust of cool air blew in. It wasn't an apology, but Martine already knew that was all she was going to get.

The dentist feeling returned on the fifteen-minute drive to school, most of which Martine spent **squirming** in her new uniform, hating the skirt and not knowing what to say to her grandmother. And it didn't **diminish** when Gwyn Thomas drove her through the gates of Caracal Junior and she saw the **hordes** of healthy, confident children who were to be her new schoolmates. They were every shade of honey, cappuccino and chocolate. None were the colour of Martine – that is to say, a sort of unhealthy grey-white. After her grandmother had left her at the door of the headmistress's office with a gruff but kindly 'Have a good day. Tendai or I will collect you at four,' she stood pressed against the wall, trying to be as **inconspicuous** as possible.

'Be with you in a mo,' called a voice when she knocked. Martine could hear someone speaking on the phone. While she waited, she took in her surroundings. Her old school, Bodley Brook, had resembled a concrete prison, with a tarmac playground and peeling beige corridors, reeking of disinfectant. The toilets had been covered in graffiti. This school didn't even look like a school. It was more like a lovely campsite. Log buildings made from glowing chestnut timber were scattered about grounds laid with emerald lawns and huge trees. Behind a wooden fence, a swimming pool sparkled.

'You can close your mouth now. We still have the same boring old lessons you had back home. You know, long division, dead kings, punctuation!'

The expression on Martine's face must have said it all, because the Cleopatra-haired vision standing in the doorway wearing wooden parrot earrings and a long purple dress laughed merrily and, pulling her into the room, added: 'Only joking. Our lessons are, of course, extremely interesting. I'm Elaine Rathmore, the headmistress, and you must be Martine. Welcome to Caracal Junior.'

From *The White Giraffe*,
Lauren St John

- Who are the characters in this part of the story?
- What are the three settings in the extract?
- Why had Martine 'been sent to Africa to live with a total stranger'?
- What is the name of Martine's new school?
- Explain the meaning of the words in **bold** as they are used in the extract.
- What do you think the author means when she writes that Martine felt 'as if she was going to the dentist', and walked downstairs 'on leaden feet'?
- Why do you think Martine's lunchbox contains sunscreen?
- Martine arrived at the game reserve the day before. Find evidence in the extract that shows her first meeting with her grandmother had not gone well.
- What is your impression of:
  a Martine's grandmother?
  b Elaine Rathmore?
- How do you think Martine was feeling:
  – when she woke up;
  – during the drive to school;
  – at school?

Snowfall

The narrator was born in the West Indies. His parents moved to England and left him with his grandmother and his uncle. Later on, he joined his parents, who he could not remember, and his brother, who he had never seen.

I was seven and I had thought that snow was like cotton wool, so I had always wondered how the children in books made snowmen stand up without the breeze blowing them away.

When my mother woke me up one morning, she said, 'There's snow darling, come and see!'

We stood at the window looking down. The tops of the parked cars were covered with thick white hair, as though they had grown old in the night. The pavement was covered with it, too, and the roof – the long row of joined-together roofs – of the opposite side of the street, everything. It was very mysterious. A giant had come and quietly laid his fluffy white towel down over the whole street and vanished again.

My mother was holding me. 'Pretty, eh?' she said. I did not answer. Instead I squirmed with shyness. I was shy of my mother. I did not know my mother, I did not know my father, and – I did not

Understanding the extract

- How old was the narrator when he first saw snow?
- How does he feel: **a** when he is with his mother and father?
  b about his brother?
- When he lived with Granny, when was the only time he was interested in his parents?
- What was the only reason he agreed to go 'Up There'?

Looking at words

Explain the meaning of these words and phrases as they are used in the extract:

a mysterious   **b** vanished   **c** scamper
d put out   **e** slightest   **f** behind my back

trust the little boy they had with them who did not talk like me and didn't seem to feel cold, who they said was my little brother.

I had looked forward to seeing my little brother. When I was going to take the plane, Granny had given me a paper bag full of sweets to bring for him. And he had sniffed and nibbled at them, screwing up his face, and handed them back to my mother.

In the night when I was falling asleep, or when I woke up in the middle of the night, then this place seemed to be a dream that I was having. It was always close and dark here, as in a dream, and there was no midday; the whole day was the same colour. And you could never just scamper out through the front door if you felt like it, you first had to pile on all those clothes that made you feel heavier than when you had got soaked in the rain.

But when I was up and about, then it was Granny and Uncle Nello who seemed to be tucked away in a dream somewhere, or in some bright yellow storybook.

Granny was both sad and happy when they'd written and said that I could go to them now. Happy for me because at last I was going Up There. They were rather put out when I announced that I wasn't going anywhere. I hadn't the slightest interest in my mother and father – only when I got parcels from them with sweets and toys; but when I had gobbled up the sweets and broken the toys or exchanged them for things my friends had, then I forgot about my mother and father until the next parcel came.

But I didn't mind going Up There to have a look at this little brother who seemed to have crept into the world behind my back, for Granny and Uncle Nello said that I had never seen him. (They also said that I *had* seen my mother and father and that they had seen me, but I knew they were only fooling me.)

And now I had come to this uncomfortable place, and I had seen my little brother, and now I was ready to go back to Granny and Uncle Nello.

From *Jeffie Lemmington and Me*, Merle Hodge

Exploring further

- The narrator describes the snow as 'cotton wool', 'thick white hair' and a 'fluffy white towel'. Which description do you think is the best? Why?
- Find evidence in the extract that suggests the narrator and his brother are not going to get along.
- Explain in your own words how the narrator feels at night.
- Why do you think the narrator thinks of Granny and Uncle Nello as being in a 'bright yellow storybook'?
- Who do you think the narrator feels is his real family? Why does he think this?

Extra

Imagine you could meet the narrator of this story.
What questions would you like to ask him?

Walkabout

Mary and Peter are on their way to their Uncle Keith in Adelaide. They are the only passengers on a small cargo plane that crashes in the Australian desert. They are the only survivors.

It was silent and dark, and the children were afraid. They huddled together, their backs to an outcrop of rock. Far below them, in the bed of the gully, a little stream flowed inland – soon to peter out in the vastness of the Australian desert. Above them the walls of the gully climbed smoothly to a moonless sky.

The little boy nestled more closely against his sister. He was trembling.

She felt for his hand, and held it, very tightly.

'All right, Peter,' she whispered. 'I'm here.'

She felt the tension ebb slowly out of him, the trembling die gradually away. When a boy is only eight a big sister of thirteen can be wonderfully comforting.

'Mary,' he whispered, 'I'm hungry. Let's have something to eat.'

The girl sighed. She felt in the pocket of her frock, and pulled out a paper-covered stick of barley sugar. It was their last one. She broke it, gave him half, and slipped the other half back in her pocket.

'Don't bite,' she whispered. 'Suck.'

Why they were whispering they didn't know. Perhaps because everything was so very silent: like a church. Or was it because they were afraid; afraid of being heard?

For a while the only sounds were the distant rippling of water over stone, and the sucking of lips around a diminishing stick of barley sugar. Then the boy started to fidget, moving restlessly from one foot to another. Again the girl reached for his hand.

'Aren't you comfy, Pete?'

'No.'

'What is it?'

'My leg's bleeding again. I can feel the wet.'

She bent down. The handkerchief that she had tied round his thigh was now draped like a recalcitrant garter over his ankle. She refastened it, and they huddled together, holding hands, looking into the powdery blackness of the Australian night.

They could see nothing. They could hear nothing – apart from the lilt of the rivulet – for it was still too early for the stirring of bush life. Later there'd be other sounds; the hoot of the mopoke, the mating howl of the dingo, and the leathery flip-flap-flip of the wings of flying foxes. But now, an hour after sunset, the bush was silent: frighteningly still: full, to the children, of terrors all the greater for being unknown. It was a far cry from here to their comfortable home in Charleston, South Carolina.

The hours meandered past, like slow, unhurrying snails. At last the boy's head dropped to his sister's lap. He snuggled closer. His breathing became slower, deeper. He slept.

But the girl didn't sleep…

From *Walkabout*, James Vance Marshall

Understanding the extract

1 Where has the plane crashed?

2 Which of the children is the oldest?

3 Where has Peter been hurt?

4 Give two examples of animals that would make noises during the night.

Understanding the words

5 Explain the meaning of these words and phrases as they are used in the extract:
   a gully   **b** vastness   **c** tension
   d ebb slowly   **e** diminishing   **f** recalcitrant
   g a far cry   **h** meandered

Exploring further

6 What impression do you get of:
   a Mary?   **b** Peter?

7 Why do you think Mary told Peter to 'suck' the barley sugar instead of biting it?

8 Why do you think she put the other half of the barley sugar in her pocket?

9 What do you think the author means when he says that the 'terrors' were 'all the greater for being unknown'?

10 Why do you think Mary didn't sleep?

Extra

Imagine you are Mary. Peter has fallen asleep. You have no food, it is night, and you are lost. Make notes on:
   • how you are feeling
   • what you are thinking about
   • what you are planning to do.

Are you convinced?

▶ **Exploring persuasive language**

You are what you eat

Do you think the food you eat affects your health? Well, scientists have given us every reason to believe that to be true, but we still seem to be ignoring them.

Walk along any high street and count the number of fast-food **establishments** that offer over-priced and under-nourishing **fare** that we are quite happy to **contaminate** our bodies with: burgers, chips, fizzy drinks and all the other items appropriately named 'junk food'.

So what should we be eating to live long and stay healthy? Let's look at just a few of the discoveries of the past few months that it would **benefit** us all to take notice of.

Take the simple almond. It has been discovered that a few almonds every day can fight cancer and heart disease. This miracle nut contains flavanoids that not only help beat cancer, but also can fight the ageing process. Not something a plate of chips can do!

And what about the apple that helps you live longer? The bitter English apple called Evesse is no longer eaten today but it should be. Its amazing ingredient, epicatechin, boosts the heart and circulation. Scientists are very excited about this discovery and you will soon be able to buy it as a juice and a sweetener.

Lifestyle

STAYHEALTHY MAGAZINE

And lastly, the humble grape. Tests have shown that within the seeds of this little fruit is an ingredient that will kill lots of leukaemia cells quickly!

So, burgers, chips and pizza, or almonds, apples and grapes? No one but a complete idiot would continue to ignore what science is telling us. And what do you notice about the healthy food? Yes, it's all natural. Not an **E-number** in sight, and no trace of the dreaded monosodium glutamate.

Do yourself a favour – and, more importantly, do your children a favour – and change your eating habits today. Set a good example and make sure your kids eat their five portions of fruit and vegetables every day. Give them a chance at a long, healthy life and bin the junk food.

The Association of Fruit and Vegetables for a Healthy Life

Other Miracle Foods

Cooked tomatoes
Help the skin fight sunburn

Blackberries
Protect against heart disease and cancer

Spinach
Combats eye disease and anaemia

Tea
Helps reduce blood pressure

› What is the writer trying to persuade you to do?

› Name three healthy and three unhealthy foods.

› Who has written the article?

› Explain the meanings of the **bold** words as they are used in the article.

› Explain in your own words what the title of the article means.

› Why do you think the writer begins with a question?

› Why do you think the writer mentions 'scientists' several times?

› Why do you think the writer uses the phrase 'no one but a complete idiot'?

› Do you think it is important to know who wrote the article or not? Explain your reasons.

› Are you persuaded by this article? Why? Why not?

J Morgan
2, Oakfields Drive
Swinnerton
SW2 6ND

19th August, 2009

Stay Healthy Magazine
233 Marathon Way
Eastfields
London
NE5 9TE

Dear Sir or Madam,

I am writing to you having read with interest the article 'You Are What You Eat' in last month's issue.

I would like to state that I am all in favour of a healthy diet and eat my five portions of fruit and vegetables every day. I have no quarrel with 'what' is said in the article but for those lovers of junk food, it is hardly going to make them change their eating habits.

Understanding the letter

- Who is writing the letter?
- To whom are they writing?
- What is the letter about?
- The letter has seven paragraphs. Write briefly what each is about.
- Why does the writer end the letter with 'Yours faithfully'?

Looking at words

Explain the meaning of these words and phrases as they are used in the letter:

a issue	**b** portions	**c** impressed
d numerous	**e** wonder drug	**f** never see the light of day
g morons	**h** vested interest	**i** scouring

If you are going to persuade people to have a healthy diet, you have to stop throwing around words like 'scientist', 'miracle ingredient', and the mysterious sounding 'epicatechin'. Do you think we will be so impressed by words we do not understand that we will think what you say must be true?

The article refers on numerous occasions to 'scientists'. Who are these scientists? What experiments have they done? How many people have these miracle ingredients been tested on? What percentage have they worked on?

Newspapers and magazines are always full of the next 'wonder drug' and 'miracle cure'. Most of them never see the light of day again.

Stop treating your readers like morons. Give us some hard facts so we can judge how much research has been done and how effective it has been. It would also help if the writers of such articles did not have a vested interest in selling their products!

I will be scouring the shops to see if the wondrous apple fruit juice ever gets to the shelves!

Yours faithfully,

J Morgan

Exploring further
- What is the purpose of the first sentence of the letter?
- How do you know that the writer is 'in favour of a healthy diet'?
- Find evidence in the letter to show that the writer is not persuaded by the article *You Are What You Eat*.

  Look for:
  - things the letter writer says that the article included
  - things the letter writer says the article did not include.
- If the writer 'spoke' the last line of the letter, what do you think the tone of voice would be?

Extra
Discuss, draft and write a group letter to persuade your school to provide a choice of fruit and vegetables every day for lunch.

Outlaw sunbeds
plea as cases of skin cancer soar

By **Lucy Johnston** and **Martyn Halle**

TANNING shops should be banned, says a leading skin charity, after revelations that children as young as eight have been using sunbeds.

Britain now has more skin cancer cases than Australia, an epidemic fuelled by an addiction to tanning.

Andrew Langford, chief executive of the Skin Care Campaign, says a whole generation of young people are raising their risk of developing skin cancer because of sunbeds.

Last week an all-party committee of MPs and peers demanded controls on tanning salons. Mr Langford wants them outlawed.

His call follows two recent events in Liverpool. One salon let an eight-year-old girl use a sunbed. Another allowed a pregnant mother to hold her three-year-old son while on a sunbed. Mr Langford said: "We were called by witnesses who couldn't believe their eyes. The sunbed industry is a disgrace.

"All evidence is that sunbeds are contributing to the skin cancer epidemic. The only way that ultraviolet light should be used is under close medical supervision to treat particular conditions." Members of the All Party Parliamentary Skin Group were shocked by new figures showing a 35 per cent rise in skin cancer over the past 10 years in Britain.

Every year 40,000 cases are diagnosed and there are 2,000 deaths.

Mark Goodfield, president of the British Association of Dermatologists, said: "Sunbeds are a major factor in the rise of skin cancer.

"Over exposure to ultraviolet light from sunbeds gives young people a 75 per cent chance of developing skin cancer as they grow older. We need to stop the under-18s going on sunbeds."

MPs want local authorities to ban sunbeds in leisure centres as this gives the false impression they are healthy.

Sunday Express, 16 November 2008

Understanding the article

1 What is the article trying to persuade people to do?

2 Who do the writers quote in the article?

3 Some people 'couldn't believe their eyes'. What had they witnessed?

4 What is the main idea of each paragraph in the article?

Understanding the words

5 Explain the meaning of these words and phrases as they are used in the article:
   a revelations   b addiction   c outlawed
   d contributing to   e medical supervision   f diagnosed

Exploring further

6 What effect do you think the writers want the headline to have?

7 Why do you think the writers quote Andrew Langford and Mark Goodfield?

8 What does Mr Langford mean when he says 'The sunbed industry is a disgrace'?

9 Why do you think the article uses figures such as '35 per cent rise in skin cancer' and '2,000 deaths'?

10 Explain in your own words why MPs want sunbeds banned in 'leisure centres'.

Extra

Write briefly to say why you are, or are not, persuaded by this article.

Long, long ago
▶ **Exploring older novels and stories**

A breakfast conversation

Roberta, Peter and Phyllis have been brought up in a comfortable and safe home in London in the early 20th century. Then one night, something happens, and afterwards their lives change dramatically.

When they came down to breakfast the next morning, Mother had already gone out.

'To London,' Ruth said, and left them to their breakfast.

'There's something awful the matter,' said Peter, breaking his egg. 'Ruth told me last night we should know soon enough.'

'Did you ask her?' said Roberta, with **scorn**.

'Yes, I did!' said Peter, angrily. 'If you could go to bed without caring whether Mother was worried or not, I couldn't. So there!'

'I don't think we ought to ask the servants things Mother doesn't tell us,' said Roberta.

'That's right, Miss Goody-goody,' said Peter, '**preach** away.'

'I'm not goody,' said Phyllis, 'but I think Bobbie's right this time.'

'Of course. She always is. In her own opinion,' said Peter.

'Oh, don't!' cried Roberta, putting down her eggspoon; 'don't let's be horrid to each other. I'm sure some **dire calamity** is happening. Don't let's make it worse!'

'Who began, I should like to know?' said Peter.

Roberta made an effort, and answered:–

'I did, I suppose, but–'

'Well, then,' said Peter, triumphantly. But before he went to school, he thumped his sister between the shoulders and told her to cheer up.

The children came home to one o'clock dinner, but Mother was not there. And she was not there at tea-time.

It was nearly seven o'clock before she came in, looking so ill and tired that the children felt they could not ask her any questions. She sank into an arm-chair. Phyllis took the long pins out of her hat, while Roberta took off her gloves, and Peter unfastened her walking-shoes and fetched her soft velvety slippers for her.

When she had had a cup of tea, and Roberta had put eau-de-Cologne on her poor head that ached, Mother said:–

'Now, my darlings, I want to tell you something. Those men last night did bring very bad news, and Father will be away for some time. I am very worried about it, and I want you to all help me, and not make things harder for me.'

'As if we would!' said Roberta, holding Mother's hand against her face.

'You can help me very much,' said Mother, 'by being good and happy and not quarrelling when I'm away' – Roberta and Peter exchanged **guilty** glances – 'for I shall be away a good deal.'

'We won't quarrel. Indeed we won't,' said everybody. And meant it, too.

'Then,' Mother went on, 'I want you not to ask me any questions about this trouble; and not to ask anybody else any questions.'

Peter **cringed** and shuffled his boots on the carpet.

'You'll promise this, too, won't you?' said Mother.

'I did ask Ruth,' said Peter, suddenly. 'I'm very sorry, but I did.'

'And what did she say?'

'She said I should know soon enough.'

'It isn't necessary for you to know anything about it,' said Mother; 'It's about business, and you never do understand business, do you?'

'No,' said Roberta. 'Is it something to do with Government?' For Father was a Government Officer.

'Yes,' said Mother. 'Now it's bed-time, my darlings. And don't you worry. It'll all come right in the end.'

'Then don't you worry either, Mother,' said Phyllis, 'and we'll all be as **good as gold**.'

Mother sighed and kissed them.

'We'll begin being good first thing to-morrow morning,' said Peter, as they went upstairs.

'Why not *now*?' said Roberta.

'There's nothing to be good about now, silly,' said Peter…

'I never wanted things to happen to make Mother unhappy,' said Roberta. 'Everything's perfectly horrid.'

Everything continued to be perfectly horrid for some weeks.

From *The Railway Children*, E. Nesbit

- Who are the characters in the story?
- Where is this part of the story set?
- What are the children talking about at breakfast?
- Where had Mother gone?
- When Mother returns, what does she:
  a tell the children?
  b ask them?
- Explain the meaning of the words and phrases in **bold** as they are used in the extract.
- What impression do you get of:
  - Phyllis?
  - Roberta?
  - Peter?
- What do you think 'happened' last night?
- Do you think the children ought to have been told what had happened to Father? Why? Why not?
- Do you think this is a modern or an old-fashioned story? Explain your reasons.

Christmas presents

*The story is set during the American Civil War in a small town in New England.
Mr March is an army chaplain, and is at the front. The main characters are his four
daughters and their mother.*

'Christmas won't be Christmas without any presents,' grumbled Jo, lying on the rug.

'It's so dreadful to be poor!' sighed Meg, looking down at her old dress.

'I don't think it's fair for some girls to have lots of pretty things, and other girls nothing at all,' added little Amy with an injured sniff.

'We've got Father and Mother, and each other, anyhow,' said Beth contentedly, from her corner.

The four young faces on which the firelight shone brightened at the cheerful words, but darkened again as Jo said sadly:

'We haven't got Father, and shall not have him for a long time.' She didn't say 'perhaps never', but each silently added it, thinking of Father far away, where the fighting was.

Nobody spoke for a minute; then Meg said in an altered tone:

'You know the reason Mother proposed not having any presents this Christmas was because it's going to be a hard winter for everyone; and she thinks we ought not to spend money for pleasure,

Understanding the extract

● What are the names of the four daughters in the story?

● Who likes:

   a drawing and goes to school?

   b reading and looks after an old lady?

   c music and does housework?

   d pretty things and teaches children?

● Explain in your own words why there won't be any presents at Christmas.

Looking at words

Explain the meaning of these words as they are used in the extract:

a army chaplain **b** contentedly **c** proposed   **d** sacrifices   **e** regretfully
f decidedly   **g** trotting   **h** fret   **i** impertinent **j** plague

when our men are suffering so in the army. We can't do much, but we can make our little sacrifices, and ought to do it gladly. But I'm afraid I don't', and Meg shook her head, as she thought regretfully of all the pretty things she wanted.

'But I don't think the little we should spend would do any good. We've each got a dollar, and the army wouldn't be much helped by our giving that. I agree not to expect anything from Mother or you, but I do want to buy Undine and Sintram for myself; I've wanted it so long,' said Jo, who was a book-worm.

'I planned to spend mine in new music,' said Beth, with a little sigh, which no one heard but the hearth-brush and the kettle-holder.

'I shall get a nice box of Faber's drawing-pencils: I really need them,' said Amy decidedly.

'Mother didn't say anything about our money, and she won't wish us to give up everything. Let's each buy what we want, and have a little fun; I'm sure we grub hard enough to earn it,' cried Jo, examining the heels of her boots in a gentlemanly manner.

'I know *I* do, teaching those dreadful children nearly all day, when I'm longing to enjoy myself at home,' began Meg in a complaining tone again.

'You don't have half such a hard time as I do,' said Jo. 'How would you like to be shut up for hours with a nervous, fussy old lady, who keeps you trotting, is never satisfied, and worries you till you're ready to fly out of the window or box her ears?'

'It's naughty to fret, but I do think washing dishes and keeping things tidy is the worst work in the world. It makes me cross; and my hands get so stiff, I can't practise…'

'I don't believe any of you suffer as I do,' cried Amy; 'for you don't have to go to school with impertinent girls, who plague you if you don't know your lessons, and laugh at your dresses, and label your father if he isn't rich, and insult you when your nose isn't nice.'

From *Little Women*, Louisa May Alcott

Exploring further
- Why do you think each of the girls silently added 'perhaps never' when they talked about their father?
- How do you know the girls are not happy about not having presents?
- Each girl is going to use her money to buy herself a present. Is this what you would have done? Why? Why not?
- Which of the four girls do you think 'suffers' the most? Explain your reasons.

Extra
Imagine Mother comes into the room at this point in the story, and the girls explain to her what they have decided to do. How does Mother react? Role-play the scene.

The Secret Garden

Mary Lennox was born and lived in India. Then her mother and father die of cholera, and she is sent to England to live with her uncle, Mr Craven, in Misselthwaite Manor. It's a huge, unfriendly place and the only people Mary sees are the household servants. One night, she hears a 'Someone' crying and goes to investigate.

…she stood in the corridor and could hear the crying quite plainly, though it was not loud. It was on the other side of the wall at her left and a few yards farther on there was a door. She could see a glimmer of light coming from beneath it. The Someone was crying in that room, and it was quite a young Someone.

So she walked to the door and pushed it open, and there she was standing in the room!

It was a big room with ancient, handsome furniture in it. There was a low fire glowing faintly on the hearth and a night-light burning by the side of a carved four-posted bed hung with brocade, and on the bed was lying a boy, crying pitifully…

The boy had a sharp, delicate face, the colour of ivory and he seemed to have eyes too big for it. He had also a lot of hair which tumbled over his forehead in heavy locks and made his thin face seem smaller. He looked like a boy who had been ill, but he was crying more as if he were tired and cross than if he were in pain.

Mary stood near the door with her candle in her hand, holding her breath. Then she crept across the room, and as she drew nearer the light attracted the boy's attention and he turned his head on his pillow and stared at her, his grey eyes opening so wide that they seemed immense.

'Who are you?' he said at last in a half-frightened whisper. 'Are you a ghost?'

'No, I am not,' Mary answered, her own whisper sounding half-frightened. 'Are you one?'…

'No,' he replied after waiting a moment or so. 'I am Colin.'

'Who is Colin?' she faltered.

'I am Colin Craven. Who are you?'

'I am Mary Lennox. Mr Craven is my uncle.'

'He is my father,' said the boy.

'Your father!' gasped Mary. 'No one ever told me he had a boy! Why didn't they?'

'Come here,' he said, still keeping his strange eyes fixed on her with an anxious expression. She came close to the bed and he put out his hand and touched her.

'You are real, aren't you?' he said. 'I have such real dreams very often. You might be one of them.'

From *The Secret Garden*, Frances Hodgson Burnett

Understanding the extract

1 How did Mary know there was 'Someone' in the room?

2 When Mary went into the room, where did she see the boy?

3 Why did she think he was crying?

4 Why did Colin think that Mary might not be real?

5 What relation was Mary to Colin?

Understanding the words

6 Explain the meaning of these words as they are used in the extract:
   a glimmer   b ancient   c brocade
   d pitifully   e ivory   f immense

Exploring further

7 How do you think:
   a Mary felt when she saw Colin?
   b Colin felt when he saw Mary?

8 Would you say Colin's room was modern or old-fashioned? Explain your reasons.

9 Why do you think:
   a Mary was 'holding her breath' as she stood by the door?
   b Colin asked, 'Are you a ghost?' when he saw Mary?

10 Why do you think Colin had 'an anxious expression' on his face when he asked Mary to come over to him?

Extra

Imagine Colin and Mary go to see Mr Craven. They ask him why he had not told them about each other. Write Mr Craven's explanation.

How to use this book

This Pupil Book consists of ten units that help to teach comprehension skills for a range of different text types and genres, including fiction, non-fiction and poetry. It can be used on its own or as part of the whole Nelson Comprehension series, including Teacher's Resource Books and CD-ROMs. Each Nelson Comprehension unit is split into three sections.

Teach

The 'Teach' section includes an illustrated text for a teacher and children to read together and discuss in class. To help guide the discussion, a series of panel prompt questions is supplied, which can be used to help model a full range of comprehension skills (such as literal understanding, inference and evaluation). Full answer guidance is supplied in the accompanying *Teacher's Resource Book*, with multi-modal whiteboard support (complete with voiceovers and a range of audio and visual features) on the CD-ROM.

Talk

The aim of this section is to get the children in small groups to practise the skills they have just learnt. Each child could take on a role within the group, such as scribe, reader or advocate. They are presented with a range of questions to practise the skills they have been learning in the 'Teach' section.

Write

The questions are followed up by a discussion, drama, role play or other group activity to further reinforce their learning. Further guidance is supplied in the *Teacher's Resource Book*, while interactive group activities to support some of the 'Talk' questions and activities are supplied on the CD-ROM.

The third section offers an opportunity to test what the children have learnt by providing a new text extract and a series of questions, which can be answered orally, as a class exercise, or as an individual written exercise. The questions are colour coded according to their type, with initial literal questions, followed by vocabulary clarification, inference and evaluation questions and then an extended follow-up activity. Full answer guidance is supplied in the accompanying *Teacher's Resource Book*, while a whiteboard questioning reviewing feature is supplied on the CD-ROM.